Story by **Michelle Myers Lackner**

Adventure Publications, Inc.
Cambridge, Minnesota

Dedication:

For my three cubs, Sara, Pete and Jo, and for Don, who made our north woods dream come true.

Images are courtesy of the Wildlife Research Institute. The author photo was provided by Don Lackner.

Book and cover design by Jonathan Norberg

10 9 8 7 6 5 4 3 2 1

Copyright 2013 by Michelle Myers Lackner
Published by Adventure Publications, Inc.
820 Cleveland Street South
Cambridge, MN 55008
1-800-678-7006
www.adventurepublications.net
All rights reserved
Printed in China

ISBN: 978-1-59193-373-1

The Story Behind the Story:

At the North American Bear Center, Dr. Lynn Rogers and Sue Mansfield, his research assistant, spend a lot of time studying bears—and changing batteries. The batteries are found in radio collars worn by the bears they study. Lily is one of those research bears.

In the fall of 2009, when Lily dug her den for the coming winter, the North American Bear Center set up a webcam inside her den. They planned to study her as she hibernated, and the researchers were amazed by what they learned. On January 22, 2010, people all over the world sat in front of their computers and watched as Lily gave birth to her cub, Hope. Researchers were able to study how a mother bear feeds, grooms and nurtures her cub in a dark den buried beneath the winter snow.

When the bears left their den, Dr. Rogers and Ms. Mansfield knew where Lily was because of the radio collar she wore. Unfortunately, there wasn't a collar small enough for a new cub like Hope.

This story is inspired by events that happened to Lily and Hope in 2010.

Note: Most of the images in the book are still shots taken from video of Lily and Hope captured by the Wildlife Research Institute. This video was created in the interest of research, not storytelling, and that makes this book unique, as it features Lily and Hope going about their natural routines. We're delighted to use this imagery to tell Hope's story.

As the snow
began to melt,

Mama peeked outside
the den and sniffed.

Her cub, Hope, opened her tiny eyes.

The bears had been curled up in their den all winter.

Now their stomachs grumbled.
It was time to search for food.

Mama nibbled buds and blooms,
crunchy shoots and chewy roots.

Mama ripped bark off of a rotted tree trunk.
She licked up wiggling grubs.

Hope looked for tasty grubs, too.

Hope followed Mama everywhere.

Mama kept Hope safe, and fed her the warm milk she needed.

One day, Mama nudged Hope up into a tree.
Then she disappeared into the woods.

Hope didn't know why Mama left her there.

She waited and waited for Mama to return.
As morning turned into afternoon, Hope grew hungry.

Hope scooted down the tree. She peered between branches and spied some sweet blueberry blossoms.

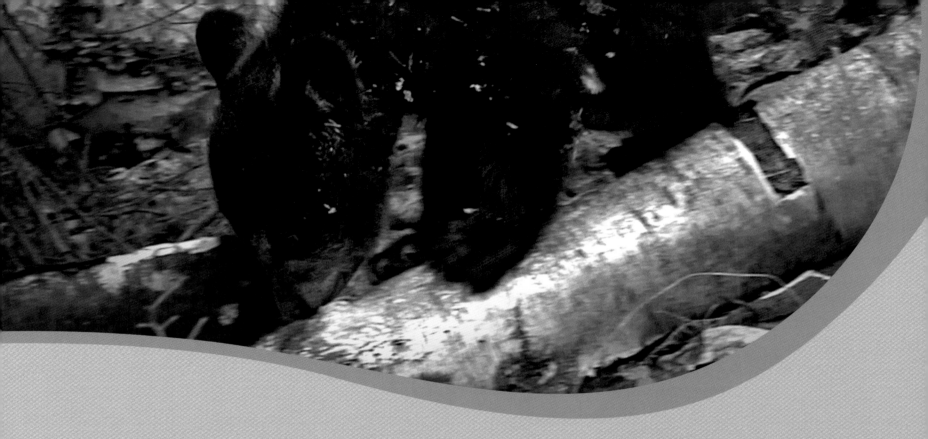

Still hungry, Hope sniffed around for more to eat,
when suddenly . . .

. . . nothing looked familiar. Where was her tree?

Hope went searching for Mama.

Meanwhile, Mama returned to the tree where she had left her cub. Where was Hope?

As twilight settled over the forest, lightning ripped across the sky and thunder rumbled in the distance. Hope needed to hide.

She climbed a sturdy tree.

The next morning, any scent of Mama had been washed away by the storm. Hope was lost!

Mama looked high and low for her cub, but she couldn't find Hope!

Days went by . . .

Without her mother's milk, Hope grew weaker and weaker.

Luckily, Hope wasn't alone in the woods.
Researchers knew that she was lost and hungry.

Hope sniffed the air. Food!

She came out of hiding and inched forward.

Hope lapped up the milk.
She gobbled up delicious
fruits and wriggling grubs.

Finally, with food in her belly, Hope could rest.

For days, the researchers left food for Hope.

Then one morning, when Hope climbed down from her hiding spot . . .

. . . a friend was waiting for her.

But Hope was afraid and tried to get away.

Strong hands grabbed her.

Hope fought and wailed
and kicked her legs.

She was pushed into a dark cage.

Hope cried while the truck rumbled and bounced down winding gravel roads.

Soon the truck stopped. The cage door sprang open. Hope bolted into the woods.

Through the thicket she saw . . . Mama!

Hope howled as she scampered over to Mama.

Hope looked up into Mama's acorn-colored eyes.
Mama gave Hope a great big hug.

Everything was better when
they were together.

Dear Reader,

Hope was indeed a cherished bear. When she got lost, researchers at the North American Bear Center near Ely, MN, were on the lookout for her. So were people living nearby. Once she was spotted, researchers raced to the site where Hope had been seen, and they set out food for her. They fed her and followed Hope's progress for days. But the researchers soon learned that without her mother's milk, Hope was growing weaker, and they feared that she would not develop properly. So Dr. Lynn Rogers and Sue Mansfield worked to reunite Lily and Hope.

Being a bear in the wilderness isn't like a story in a picture book. It can be a hard life. Bears have to stay away from danger (including other bears) and they have to try to find a place to live, which is difficult since wild areas are shrinking because of human development. If a wild bear gets sick, there is no veterinarian for him to visit. If a cub gets hungry, there isn't a grocery store where she can buy blueberries or grubs. And a bear needs to eat a lot to grow, stay healthy and get ready to hibernate. When bears hibernate, they live off the stored fat from all the berries, roots and other foods they've found in the woods.

Bears also need to worry about hunters. In the fall of 2011, Hope slipped out of her radio collar, which identified her as a research bear. Sadly, Hope was mistakenly shot by a hunter who didn't know who she was.

I look at it this way: when Hope was a cub and lost, she likely would have starved to death. Luckily, researchers at the NABC were looking out for her. Dr. Rogers and Ms. Mansfield fed Hope and reunited her with her mama. (Only experienced researchers should attempt to feed a bear.) Hope may not have survived without their help. And because of their help, Lily and Hope were able to spend a wonderful summer together. Then in the fall, when Lily dug her den to hibernate, Hope snuggled in with her mama.

During that winter, two new cubs were born. Hope was crawled on, had her ears nibbled and had to share Lily's attention. She had two new playmates and was a terrific big sister. In spring, when the snow melted and the loons returned to the north woods, Lily and Hope scrambled out of their den with the new cubs.

The story of Lily and Hope has many more twists and turns than are told in this book. In reality, they were separated several times. Why does this happen? Will a mama bear go mark her territory and leave her cub to wait for her? Could she be scared out of her territory by another bear?

Researchers like Dr. Rogers and Ms. Mansfield are trying to unravel these questions—and more. We need to support them to learn about our bear neighbors. Through understanding and education, we have a better chance of peacefully sharing the wild places with bears.

The North American Bear Center is devoted to studying bears, understanding them and educating people about them. By purchasing this book, you're supporting their work—and bears! If you want to know more about the amazing work of Dr. Rogers and the NABC, please check out www.bear.org. There, you'll learn more about the lives of many wild and wonderful bears. There are updates on new bears, old bears, and new discoveries about them. The website also includes fun facts about bears and stories about the bears that the NABC is studying; it's almost like taking a trip to the north woods! If you're ever in Ely, Minnesota, stop by the NABC and say "Hello!" to some of our wild neighbors.

A bear hug from me—Michelle Myers Lackner, Ely, MN

L to R:
Michelle Myers Lackner
Dr. Lynn Rogers, Founder, NABC
Sue Mansfield, Biologist

About the Author:

Michelle Myers Lackner found the wilderness and the community she'd been searching for near Ely, Minnesota. She has written numerous articles, essays and poems for magazines. This is her second book for children.

Michelle first met Hope as a little cub in the tree in this very picture. On a quiet spring morning, she heard a loud ripping sound. Was someone attacking her kayaks? No, it was Lily. She was huge, but she easily climbed the big, old white pine in Michelle's backyard. Shards of bark flew everywhere. Higher and higher Lily climbed, and then Michelle saw a small somebody peeking out from behind a thick branch. It was Hope—the tiny, timid cub waiting for her mama. The author met Lily and Hope in her backyard and had the unique privilege of observing Lily and her cub in the wild.

Once afraid of bears, Michelle learned from the NABC that her wild neighbors aren't a threat to her safety, they're simply looking for food. Michelle and her husband, Don, now happily share the woods with them.